The Ethical Exit

Transition Your Work and Love your Life

Jeanne Boschert

Copyright © 2015
Jeanne Boschert

All rights reserved. No part of this book may be reproduced in any form without permission in writing from the author. Reviewers may quote brief passages in reviews.

ISBN: 978-1-942646-10-5

DISCLAIMER
No part of this publication may be reproduced or transmitted in any form or by any means, mechanical or electronic, including photocopying or recording, or by any information storage and retrieval system, or transmitted by email without permission in writing from the author.

Neither the author nor the publisher assumes any responsibility for errors, omissions, or contrary interpretations of the subject matter herein. Any perceived slight of any individual or organization is purely unintentional.

Brand and product names are trademarks or registered trademarks of their respective owners.

Cover Design, Interior Design and Back Cover Photograph: John H. Matthews

Interior Author Photograph: Suzette Osborn

Editing: Grace Kerina

Advance Praise

Here are what some of the people are saying about Jeanne, her work and this book.

"Jeanne Boschert is the most humble and gorgeous soul I have come across, with a God-given ability to quickly and simply inspire and empower women to get out of their own way...and LIVE their dream life! She touches everyone she comes across, with her "real" approach, jammed packed full of wisdom, humor and love. If you are on a life-quest, ready for a shift and searching for answers, The Ethical Exit will guide you on a life-changing journey; changing your path and altering your perspective in the most beautiful and impactful way. With Jeanne's coaching and inspiration, you will know how you really want to show up in this world and will start to live the life you were destined to live. If you only read one book this year, make it The Ethical Exit and take control."

Beth Hudson
Founder & President, Answers For Women
www.answersforwomen.ca

"Ethical Exit tackles a tough challenge: making a positive career change without burning bridges. Jeanne Boschert shares powerful stories, tools, and strategies that will help you to take responsible action today toward your dreams of tomorrow."

Pam Slim
CEO of Pam Slim
Author: Body of Work, Leaving Cubicle Nation
www.pamslim.com

"If you are secretly longing for something more in your professional life, this book will show you how to identify and revise your career path to dramatically increase your fulfillment and create success that is an authentic expression of you! Jeanne is magnetic as she demystify the process of having exactly what you want by embracing and shifting your longing into a life of truth, integrity and joy."

Patti Keating
The Entrepreneur Unleashed

"If you are a coach, you need to read this book to understand your clients' journeys. If you plan to leave your job any time soon, you need this book as your companion. Coach Jeanne Boschert shares her personal journey of successfully making the leap to her heart's highest calling -- and she'll show you how to, too!"

> Debbie Phillips
> Life and Executive Coach
> Founder, Women on Fire®

"I believe the world is in dire need of women willing to step up and in their role as Freedom Leaders. God designed us to be free thinkers but we have allowed society to suppress us. I ask you to consider your own personal freedom. How free are you emotionally, spiritually, and physically? It's time we as women lead the way into the free world. It's our duty to show others the path to their destiny."

> Kellie Keutcha
> Owner of The Omnipresent Soul

"For everyone who silently questions there is more to life, for everyone who is afraid to make the big leap, there is an angel to guide you! And her name is Jeanne Boschert. Her non-nonsense approach, years of experience and masterful coaching put a practical framework to magical dreaming. She takes the plunge out of making a big change by guiding you through a nuts and bolts, tried and true framework. Working with Jeanne will empower you to remove the distraction of drama and the burden of risk out of transforming your life and doing the work you are most needed to do in the world!"

Beth Wonson
Leadership and Executive Coach
Beth Wonson Consulting
www.bethwonson.com

"Jeanne Boschert offers kind but firm, loving guidance when you are looking to truly shift your life, business, and finances. Together, we're accelerating the pace of my business growth. I'm tracking expenses more closely than ever before, and being much more mindful about the purchases I make. I am totally confident that with Jeanne's help I will clear my debt and rock my business, catapulting myself to a higher level than I have been aspiring to reach for a while now! Jeanne calls upon her life coach training, her extensive success in the business world, and her own personal financial success to guide her clients in creating their best lives. Every coach needs a coach, and I am blessed to have Jeanne as mine!"

Lisa Powell Graham, MPA
Martha Beck Certified Life Coach
www.AwesomeGoddessPosse.com

"There is no one more qualified to write this book! Having been an observer, cheerleader and sometime participant in Jeanne's personal and professional journey I have to say that her pathway from there to here has had all the markings of an interstate system- there have been exits along the way but no stop lights! Each exit has been, in reality, only an entrance to somewhere else! There are definite skills required for that kind of traveling: a good (internal) compass, steady steering, good timing, and smooth execution. Jeanne has all of these! Who better to follow down the road? In "Ethical Exits" she's shared her proven and time-worn map with us! Don't know about you, but I'm in for this road trip!"

Marilyn Cullum
Licensed Professional Counselor

I want to dedicate this work to everyone who has ever felt the desire to do more in their life than just the expected. To anyone who has wanted to play "bigger" but just did not know how, and to every brave soul who has made an Ethical Exit, God bless you for paving my path.

I want to always acknowledge my husband Bill, who has supported my dreams since day one no matter how crazy he thought they were, and to my children and family who inspire me to be a better version of myself every day. I love you all.

Table of Contents

FOREWORD I
INTRODUCTION V

CHAPTER 1
THE END IS THE BEGINNING 1

CHAPTER 2
IT'S NOT YOUR BOSS'S FAULT 10

CHAPTER 3
REALITY CHECK 29

CHAPTER 4
READING ALL THE SIGNS 41

CHAPTER 5
YES YOU CAN! BUT SHOULD YOU? 63

CHAPTER 6
PLANNING TO LEAVE 73

CHAPTER 7
WHEN THE EXIT IS NOT YOUR IDEA 83

CHAPTER 8
INACTION CAN BE YOUR ENEMY 97

CONCLUSION 111
ACKNOWLEDGEMENTS 113
ABOUT THE AUTHOR 121
ABOUT DIFFERENCE PRESS 123
OTHER BOOKS BY DIFFERENCE PRESS 127
THANK YOU 129

Foreword
by Susan Hyatt

When did I know that I needed to quit my job as a residential real estate agent?

Maybe it was that one time I curled up under my desk at the office – wearing that hot pink power suit that I bought because I thought I was "supposed" to – bent over in a fetal position, sobbing.

Or maybe it was that other time I slumped down, in tears, on the dock near the lake – because it was Sunday night, we were packing up, and I didn't want to go home. Because home meant bed. Bed meant waking up. Waking up meant Monday morning.

And Monday morning meant… my job.

Yeah. Looking back, those were probably two pretty big clues.

Even though I knew that real estate wasn't the right career for me, I felt completely shackled to my profession – for so many reasons.

My family relied on my income. My husband, who also happened to work in commercial real estate, *loved* his work, and I didn't want to admit to him that I didn't feel the same way. Plus, there was an even bigger problem: if I quit real estate, what would I do next? I didn't have a specific game plan, right at the beginning. That, more than anything else, is what held me back. I was scared of the unknown.

It took time, therapy, and intensive life coaching before I felt ready to hand in my notice.

On my final day at work, I left all of my belongings right there, at my desk, because I couldn't stand the thought of staying *one* extra minute to pack up my things properly.

I actually hired a local teenager to go into the office, after hours, to collect everything for me. Once he brought my belongings from my old office to my house, I instructed him to put everything in the garage. I didn't unpack those boxes for *years*.

It was *that* bad.

So, why I am telling this miserable story?

It's so miserable it's actually almost comical, now, nearly ten years later, because my life is so staggeringly different. Today: I run a business I love, filled with clients I adore, working at a pace that feels sane and humane. That pink power suit? It's decomposing somewhere in a landfill. Sorry, Planet Earth. Never again. And good riddance.

So.

The reason I am telling this miserable story, about what it felt like to leave my corporate job, is that looking back I see that I made the process of "leaving" so much harder and more complicated than it needed to be.

I made it harder… by lying to myself and to others. ("No really." sniffle-choke-sob. "It's just allergies.")

I made it harder… by allowing fear to cloud my intuition. ("I'm so terrified of losing my income I can't even THINK about what kind of career I might prefer.")

I made it harder… by making assumptions about how people in my community would respond. ("I can't tell anyone I'm planning to quit. They'll all think… I'm a quitter.")

Basically, I made the entire process of "exiting" my corporate career as hard as it could possibly be. If a book like this one had existed, back then? I would have snatched it off the bookshelves and poured over it with a triple-shot latte. It might have saved me a lot of torment. It might have given me hope. Hope… and a plan.

A plan to exit my job while keeping my health, sanity, professional connections, income and dignity intact.

For all of the power-suited-fetal-position-sobbers out there?

Know that… you're going to be OK. You will survive this transition. You are stronger and more resilient than you realize. There is so much waiting for you on the other side.

I am living proof. The people profiled in this book? Their stories are proof, too.

It sounds unbelievably *cliché*, but if we can do it? So can you.

And thanks to the book that you're holding in your hands – or flicking through on your e-reader – right now?

You get to skip about 80% of the drama that I went through. (Lucky you!)

Here's to the next chapter of your life and career.

Here's to discovering work that you really, truly love to do.

Introduction

I am so glad you've chosen to join me on this journey – to treat your professional life with integrity as you create a life you love. I've lived a life like many of you have: trying to find purpose as a traveling corporate career chaser. Including the search for meaning in empty hotel rooms and lonely airports as I waited for yet another delayed or canceled flight; the feelings of wanting to be in my own bed but when I get there it feels unfamiliar; working really hard and still finding myself searching, and wondering why I continue to go through the motions.

Does any of this sound like your life?

It was mine. I found myself feeling as if I were watching my life go by, and I was not even an active participant. So I decided to examine what I truly wanted, and then set my intentions to make it happen.

This book is how I share my journey. Please accept it as my personal gift to you.

My hope is that by the end of this book, you will have uncovered the answers to some of your life's quest. I've been that person, looking for answers and options, and I know how that can feel. I've also been that person who felt there were answers for everyone except me. This is my simple and humble attempt to share with you a small portion of a great big story about how I was able to make the shift – and realize that the life that I always wanted really *is* possible.

I feel it's important that I share a little bit about myself, for those of you who don't know me. I'm a southern girl with southern roots, who grew up eating fried chicken on Sundays with a big glass of sweet tea. I was always taught that there is a right way to do everything, and as long as I follow my heart, all will be ok. At our house, the Golden Rule was applied to everyone, and truth and trust were as important as air. This set of core values was a gift as well as a curse for me, for many years. Those beliefs and that sense of duty and responsibility kept me chained to a job where I was unhappy and unfulfilled. Those same core beliefs were also what I relied on to *free* me. My truth was the gift that allowed me to create a plan, and know that I could change my situation, to create a life I love – and to do it responsibly and without regret.

I had a great job, a supportive husband, and was making great money. The company I worked for had a mission I believed in, and it followed every value that was part of my core beliefs. My boss was great and offered me plenty of opportunities to express myself in my work. But something was still missing. I found myself longing for and believing that there had to be more to life than just a job. I felt that for me there was a greater purpose. I looked at different positions within the company, and I took on many new roles, hoping that would be the golden gift that would give me contentment in my life. It didn't happen.

To solve the mystery of why I felt this deep discontentment, I went on a personal journey. I discovered that my insecurity about leaving my job had nothing to do with my belief in creating a new life for myself. My inability to leave was tied to my need to do it with such a level of integrity and responsibility that it would not rock the rest of my world.

At the time I began this journey, I had a daughter in college, my husband and I were caring for aging parents, and I had made financial commitments I felt needed to be maintained along with any work roles I chose. I wasn't willing to sacrifice my family or their needs for my contentment. But a part of me knew I'd never be satisfied until I was able to create a plan for change that I could execute comfortably. My journey was one of freedom and planning to be able to feel that my decisions were done with integrity and responsibility. This is how the Ethical Exit was born.

Hopefully, if you face the same fears and challenges I faced – regarding how you can create a life you love and do it the right way – reading *The Ethical Exit* will help you clarify your life and launch your goals. You may find that for you interjecting more of what you love into what you currently do will be enough. Explore with me what your very best life can look like.

In each chapter throughout the book, I'll share my journey, both the good and the bad times, and walk you through descriptions of the process I used and the exercises that go with them. You'll read actual case studies of people just like you that will hopefully bring you additional support and clarify the fact that if others can create a life they love you can too.

Sometimes, what people *think* they want – going into this journey – is not what they end up creating. The stories I share will allow you to see what to expect along the way as you experience the consequences and outcomes that can occur on your own journey.

As we explore options in these next few chapters, understand that the path I'll share with you was not easy. It did not come without internal battles, intentional planning, or emotional bruising at times. But, I can say in the end it was worth everything to have a life that allows me the freedom to implement my passion for helping people every day. I invite you to join me.

Chapter 1
The End is the Beginning

In Steven Covey's best-selling business and self-help book, *The 7 Habits of Highly Effective People*, he describes habits that are essential in making paradigm shifts in our lives. One of his premises is that we should begin with the end in mind. It's important to envision what we want in the future, so we can make choices in the present that will lead us there. This concept was one of the first things I wanted to do as I began my journey to design and build a life and career that would be both fulfilling and rewarding. I had to get a clear vision regarding the ingredients I wanted to include in my transition and my new life.

I grew up in a small southern town with a strong sense of community. I had a large southern family grounded in wise values that didn't have to be spoken often, because we saw them in action every day. My parents and grandparents lived them. That southern upbringing deeply influenced my core character and beliefs about life. I came to understand that truth is everything, authentic is the only way, and when you die, your integrity is all you will leave as part of your legacy. Those core beliefs have been the foundation for this book, and for the process I want to share with you, so you can create a life that allows you to be happy and fulfilled – while remaining ethical about the process.

WANTING MORE
It seems that I have had a job my whole life. I've worked since I was 13 years old. First as a babysitter, then as an assistant in a dentist office while in high school. I had my first child at 19, my second at 21, and went to school and worked full-time to secure a degree in nursing. I've always felt a huge sense of responsibility for family and work, and being a contributing member of society, as defined by my southern culture. When I began to realize that I wanted to veer off the traditional course of what was

expected, I ignored it for many years, as I was busy being a very young wife and mother. I thought the longing and that unnamed desire deep within me that kept poking and prodding me would go away with time.

One of my greatest moments of anxiety was when I realized that the desire for something more in my life was not going away. I had tried everything to satisfy it. I'd tried to feed it, I'd tried to work it out, I'd tried to run from it, and I'd tried my best to ignore it. But no matter how hard I tried, I could not get that "soul hole" to go away.

Move forward several years, and I found myself much older, with a great job, and a life other people might envy. I'd climbed the ladder and was making a great comfortable income. I had a truly awesome team of coworkers and work friends. I was blessed with a truly amazing, motivating, and inspiring boss. And my personal life was written with that same storybook ending: my kids are awesome, my husband supportive, and on the outside life appeared to be great. And yet, I could not stop asking myself: "*What is wrong with me?*"

I searched for answers, but seemed to always come to the same conclusion: *I am just not content or satisfied. There has got to be more to life than this. Is this all that I am meant to do?* I didn't really think so. I had always felt that there was a bigger life for me, something more I was supposed to do, a greater purpose that sometimes felt way too big for me to pursue. My dreams and purpose scared me at times, but I wasn't sure why. I continued to search for meaning because I needed my life to matter, and I knew I was supposed to make a difference. My faith played a tremendous role in my search for the significant life that I am now blessed to live.

If you're reading this book, chances are you've felt this same longing: *There's got to be more to life than this.* If you're like me, success by the world's standard was no longer a motivator for you. When you were younger, you may have thought that if you could only get the promotion or the new job or the perfect house or the new car or _____ (you fill in the blank), you would then be happy, only to find, after you got all those things, you still felt as if something was missing.

Now you're past middle age, successful in your personal and professional life, and realize that the longing is still there: *How do I fill it? How do I satisfy what I don't understand?* These are questions I've routinely heard from clients and coworkers for many years, more times than I care to count.

My southern classic response, "Bless their heart," was not making my clients' and coworkers' emptiness and longing for a different life any better, and it didn't help mine either. That unfulfilled need only strengthened my own desire to create a life and work that I loved. It was this deep longing that lead me to create the Ethical Exit. I'll share with you the method that allowed me to walk away from my secure job, and dig deep into who I was and what I wanted my ideal life to be like.

I know if you're reading this you have some of those same thoughts: *I'm unhappy in my current role. I feel unfulfilled, and wonder if there's more to life than just going through the motions.* I assure you that you can totally redesign your life to have more of what you want, and remove what makes you feel chained, drained, and bored.

GO TO YOUR HAPPY PLACE

Fantasize with me for a moment. If you could create your ideal life, what would it look like? Who would be in your life? What would you be doing? How would you show up in the world? Is there a dream you've always had, but maybe put on hold, that you still long to accomplish? I'd like you to really give some time to your dreams and desires and flush them out. It is in the process of defining what your ideal life looks like that you can start to explore ways to get there.

As a coach, this was one of the first tools I started to use. The answers I've heard to these questions about dreams have been very eye-opening. There have been many times when I have passed out the ideal life worksheets, and people began to cry. When I saw this response, I initially didn't know what to say, but when I asked one reader in a very small intimate group what was causing her emotional response, she said, "I have no idea." She went on to share with us how her life had been so busy for so long – with trying to climb the ladder and be successful in her career – that she had lost the ability to even see life any differently. She had allowed herself to get to a place where she no longer even knew what would make her happy any more.

You may be reading this and thinking, *Gosh, what a sad story*, but the truth is that an emotional reaction to reconnecting with dreams is far more common than you might imagine. I hear such stories all the time, and there are moments when I'm so aware that *this* is why I am here and writing this book. It has become my mission to create ways to help people who find themselves lost in their own life.

If you want to start exploring your own ideal life using what I call a Longing List, you can download it from my website at www.jeanneboschert.com/downloads. There will be additional goodies throughout the book that will be in that same online location so you can easily access them, along with other supportive information for your questioning. If you'd like me to guide you through any of these processes, please feel free to contact me or set up a time for us to talk.

YOUR LONGING LIST

I've used techniques as a coach over the years to help clients reach a level of clarity about what makes them happy. One of them is the Longing List. I use it with individuals and in groups to encourage my clients to revisit what it is that evokes a feeling of passion. I have them to make a list of things they long for, things they're completely passionate about, which can be anything. The result is their unique and personal list for their ideal life. I'll have them use that list of ingredients as they begin to create a life for themselves that is satisfying and provides them with a new sense of joy.

Some of the common themes that come up for people in their Longing Lists almost always involve rest, relaxation, travel, family, and success – as defined by them. I would consider many of the things people include to be retreats for the soul, of various types. As I've looked at vision boards and Longing Lists for years, I've seen that we all long for things that reflect being able to slow down our own lives and being able to include things that bring passion for what we love back into the equation.

It's helpful to organize your Longing List into wants, needs, and non-negotiable categories to be included in your most passionate life.

Once you get really clear about what you want, need, and consider non-negotiable, it makes adding those ingredients to your life much easier. You want success, but at what price? What are you willing to sacrifice to get it?

My non-negotiable included a plan for my responsible financial transition. Then my *wants* were the cherry on my whipped cream for my ideal life plan.

Now I don't want you to think for one minute that this is going to be like any of those strategy or execution plans where you can put your team together to work on in your traditional corporate killer fashion, then create a tight timeline and do a kick-off! Hold on, killer, this is your *life*. We need to take care of *you*, and do this in the most responsible and ethical way that not only honors you, but also feels like it happens at a pace you can handle.

Go ahead and try it out.

WORKSHEET: LONGING LIST

Make a list of all the ingredients that you want or that make you happy. What types of things get you excited and that you think are fun. This will include things that you have always wanted to do. Work with your coach to identify how these can be incorporated into your life to increase your satisfaction and feelings of contentment.

Beside each one check if it is a Have, Want to or Need to.

	HAVE TO	WANT TO	NEED TO

Chapter 2
It's Not Your Boss's Fault

I've already shared with you that I had a great job, making a really great salary, in a company with a mission and vision totally aligned with my core values. I had friends at work, was doing work I loved, and felt like I'd earned the respect of my peers and co-workers. Yet I spent many sleepless nights lying awake trying to figure out what it was about my current situation that left me feeling as if I were literally lost in my own life.

There were times I felt like I was watching everything play out on the outside, but had no real connection to what was occurring around me. I could not for the life of me come up with any logical or factual answers to this situation that made sense. By all social standards, I should have been on top of the world. I should have been satisfied, happy and loving life. The sad reality was that I wasn't, and I desperately wanted to know why.

I was packing my suitcase one more time to catch a flight to Orlando for a business trip. I'd only been home for two days this time, but it was time to repack and go again. You know you have a hectic travel schedule when you keep two suitcases packed. I kept one suitcase packed with all my black coordinating clothing, and another suitcase that contained a totally brown wardrobe. Don't laugh! It was one of my tricks for trying to be efficient and productive, but still able to ensure I had the right shoes and accessories. But that's another story... so back to the point.

I'd been given a position many of my coworkers probably secretly envied: I worked as director of operations for the home health branch of the company, and part of my job was to transition and onboard a group of newly acquired sites into our corporate culture. My current assignment offered me the luxury of spending the winter in Florida. Yep, I was getting paid to be a snowbird, and would be in Florida for most of the winter. Several coworkers had jokingly asked if they could go along to assist me. I live in Memphis, Tennessee, so the thought of warm sunny days and beach walks was quite glamorous to most of my friends. After all, they were going to be stuck in freezing snow and below normal temperatures. But I did not share that same joy. As I was packing and moaning about leaving my family again, an overwhelming realization came to me. *My discontentment was not my boss's fault!*

The company had been more than gracious to me. Everyone had been totally supportive and I had absolutely no logical reason to complain. So why did I find myself wanting to whine about having to go back to Florida? Every fiber of my being was grateful for my job, yet I was still dissatisfied.

My new understanding of myself, that day, led to the discovery that my level of discontent had nothing to do with any external factors. It had everything to do with ME! Bless my heart, I'd just had one of the most simple but revolutionary, life-changing, eye-opening events I'll ever experience: This was really *all* about *me*.

THE BLAME GAME

I've worked in corporate environments for many years, and one thing that's clear is that there's no shortage of people knowing how to play the blame game. In some companies, it's the preferred sport. The corporate world's attitude, it seemed, was that everything is everyone else's fault. *That other department dropped the ball. The second shift didn't do their job. If it weren't for that, this would not have happened. Waa Waa Waa! BLAH BLAH BLAH!!* Really?

Here's the most painful piece of reality that I need to share with you in this entire book, so let's just get it out of the way: *Your discontent and unhappiness are not your boss's fault!*

I've come to believe that we all bear a certain level of responsibility that we're sometimes unwilling to admit. In every situation that rises as a problem, one of three things has occurred:

1. We caused the problem. This can be the direct result of something we did or did not do that triggered the event.

2. We participated in the problem. This can be by joining in and continuing on with the conversation or by continuing the behavior or action that was started.

3. We allowed the problem. This is the result of continuing the situation or lack of action to stop the situation.

Asking these three questions related to your level of involvement is useful for taking problems and dissecting them to see exactly what role you have been playing, and to begin to take more responsibility for your contributions to the situation.

WORKSHEET: RESPONSIBILITY FACTOR

Write the last 2=3 situations or challenges that upset you. Write what you feel is your responsibility. Did you somehow cause the problem? Did you participate in the problem or allow a problem? Your coach will work with you to identify how these thoughts and actions identified could be blocking our progress. **Example**: Rumor or gossip about a coworker that resulted in HR involvement... Did you start rumor, participate in rumor or allow rumor and do nothing to stop it?

	CAUSE	PARTICIPATE	ALLOW

I'd been good at coaching and teaching others to take responsibility, but had not done it in my own life, and that was gut-wrenching. I found myself feeling like a hypocrite by totally going against my own core values.

So now that I was aware that my discontentment was mine and mine alone to own, the question that began to run through my mind like a Broadway marquee was: *what are you going to do about it?*

As I reflected on how to get myself out of the trap that I was calling my life, I ran across a book that nailed exactly what I felt like was my problem was: Ben Arment's book *The Dream Year*.

In his book, Ben Arment described the battle that was going on within my soul. It was a launching point for me to redefine my life. He wrote, "We are motivated by two conflicting types of fears in life: the fear of failure, and the fear of insignificance. What we endeavor to do in life is determined by which fear is the strongest."

Arment's description of his own experience seemed similar to what I was battling internally:

"Throughout my life, I have gone back and forth between the two fears, as I've forgotten what it's like on the other side. I have been terrified at the prospect of losing my life savings and I've been frightened at the toiling of my whole life away on other people's dreams. But I've made my choice. I have decided which one I will fear the most. I want to do something significant with my life. I choose the fear of insignificance."

Arment goes on to say that we each must choose for ourselves which fear will be the strongest – failure or insignificance. He explained that if we don't chose for ourselves, it will be chosen for us, and the fear of failure will win that battle every time.

I was definitely in a war with my two fears. My fear of failure had ruled my life up to this point, but now my fear of insignificance was getting stronger and definitely winning the battle. This battle was the cause of my discontent and unhappiness. I wanted to be doing more with my life, for a cause greater than myself. I longed to play bigger!

WHAT DOES MORE MEAN?

I've consulted and coached for years, and I hear – over and over – that people have this same sense of wanting more for their life. The repeating theme is wanting to give more, do more, and be more in their own lives. I hear stories of people missing their children's events, not having enough time, and losing a sense of connection to those they love. My clients find themselves eating alone in restaurants, living in their cars, or in airports. Their wardrobe for the day is reduced to what they can pack in a carry on suitcase. I have heard these complaints at every company I have ever been associated or worked with. I sometimes see this unspoken discontent in people's eyes. The spark has gone. There are distant, almost absent stares around the corporate boardroom table. No one is paying attention. Everyone is on their phone or computer, only pretending to listen to a speech they care nothing about because they've heard it all before. They're being promised that things are going to change. The sad reality is that it never does.

Depressing, right? So why do people stay?

What I've uncovered over the years is that people stay for a variety of reasons, but at the core of all of them we find that they've let their fear of failure dominate their lives. Fear stops us from make the leap, taking the chance, reaching out, and trusting ourselves. People who let fear dominate their life will remain in a state of status quo and live their lives being comfortably uncomfortable.

Can you relate to any of this? Are you able to see yourself in any of what I have talked about?

I am going to challenge you and encourage you to keep reading. There will be moments when you might think, *OMG! She's been snooping at my planner, because she totally gets where my life is.* And then there will be moments when you think, *Ouch that hurts!* But my goal for you is that at the end of this book you will have realized that the life that you want for yourself is totally possible, especially when you work as hard on your own dreams as you do to fulfill everyone else's.

As a nurse for many years, I've witnessed firsthand the physical effects that can occur in people who've operated their entire professional life in the fast lane. The chronic effects of stress and bad habits lead to things like high blood pressure, ulcers, excess weight, depression, and even suicides. The results of poor habits like eating on the go, not making time for exercising, lack of sleep, and chronic levels of stress complicate the issues and prevent the living of a quality life. People allow their fears to trap them into a level of existence that only serves to harm. Fear can destroy homes, families, relationships, health, and eventually lives. Yet millions of people are choosing to keep this pace every day. Humans are not meant to run on a hamster wheel.

Can you see yourself, or a small part of you, in any of these scenarios?

I'm here to assure you that you're not alone. There are millions of people out there just like you. Unfortunately, many will choose to stay and be comfortable with doing life on autopilot. You can do something different.

Since I made my own Ethical Exit, I've been amazed at the number of people who've come to

for taking action, but to that
say I'm now concerned that t
jobs! As they try to balance w
what they hate, I'm conc
outcome. It has been my
southern farm girl who's
before, this could likely result
pain in the behind.

The question I'm asked
explore a life more meaning
while still maintaining the s
that I have?" I'll answer with
in the beginning of my time c
happened to me unconscious
box adventures led me to
longing to experience and cor
more significant way.

LIVING WITH SIGNIFIGAN
As part of my ongoing quest
missing in my life, I volunt

skills to go to Indonesia in 2004, following the devastating tsunami that reportedly took over 283,000 lives. I remember my feelings very clearly as I left on that journey. I was anxious and afraid of what I might see or find there. I was going into a country that was unknown to me, and to greater increase my level of fear, I was going to enter a country that had previously been closed to the western world for over a decade. The threat of terror was extremely high, and the U.S. was still trying to make sense of the attacks of September 11, 2001.

Despite my fear and level of uncertainty, knowing that I was possibly entering into danger, my sense of purpose and clarity about what I was doing had never been greater. I was so drawn to it – the knowledge that this was exactly what I was supposed to be doing – that it was eerie. While it didn't make sense to many of my family and friends, my internal fear, of not showing up in life in this way, outweighed my external fear of harm.

My choice to go to Indonesia to help led me to encounter people who thought I'd lost my mind. I also had to filter the voices in my own head that could think of a thousand reasons to stay at home. I had to listen to the pull to this purpose, because it was about to expose the very best *me* that I'd ever been.

That trip changed my life. It was a perfect example of my fear of failure being overruled by my fear of insignificance.

Mark Twain once said that "The two most important days in life are the day that you were born, and the day that you discover why."

Nothing can replace the feeling of realizing that you're showing up at just the right place at just the right time and for all the right reasons. The sense of alignment that comes from living with significance is undeniable.

THE BEST ME
To find that same level of courage, purpose, and commitment – when it came to creating more of it in my new best life back at home – I had to be able to remember the very best *me* I could be. I had to tap into those same feelings: fear of the unknown, while continuously trying to define my clarity and sense of purpose. Because of having done that, my new life has a greater purpose.

As you begin to define and create your new future, you'll need to do the work of defining what you really want in life. What makes you feel that you're functioning as the highest form of *you*?

I've created an exercise called The Best Me that I use with my clients, in which I ask them to recognize a time in which they felt brave and strong and courageous in spite of fear. When you can pull and deliver that kind of energy, passion, and drive up to the conscious level, you're able to recreate it again and apply it to what you want in your life. When you're able to tap into that drive, it's easier to make those first steps.

If you want to start exploring your own ideal life using the Best Me exercise along with other supportive information on my website at www.jeanneboschert.com/downloads.

WORKSHEET: BEST ME!

Identify a peak time when you felt that life was especially rewarding and poignant for you. This can be a specific event or specific time that you felt that life was rewarding and left you fulfilled or satisfied you.

Where were you?

Who was with you?

What was happening?

What was it that made it so special?

What does this say about what is important, fulfilling and meaningful to you?

Your coach will work with you to identify your thoughts and goals and how you can progress toward each of them.

I have a client we will call Sarah. She's miserable in her job; she feels she's been overlooked for promotions and has been assigned to a travel schedule that looks like something from a Delta airlines website. She feels that all the added road and travel time is impacting her relationships. Sarah has always played in the safe zone of life, and prides herself on never taking risk financially. She's played by the rules, but feels that life has not been fair, because the results have not rewarded her actions.

It was important for me to first help Sarah see that even though her frustrations had several outside factors that made them appear to be caused externally, ultimately her hating her job was her own responsibility. (Remember the three questions in the section where I realized my dissatisfaction was not my boss's fault?) Sarah had not voiced her dissatisfaction to her supervisor, or discussed her feeling that her travel schedule was excessive. Because she'd always followed the rules, she felt that those were the only options she had.

During one of our conversations, I asked Sarah, "What are you afraid will happen if you say something to your boss about this?" Her reply was, "They might fire me." To that, I replied, "So? And what else?" Her breakthrough came at the moment she realized that being fired from a job she hated might actually be a gift. She's then have time to decide for herself what she really wanted instead of going along with what she felt she had to do. That moment was freeing for Sarah. As a result, she discussed her concerns without reservation with her supervisor. Alterations in job duties were arranged, and Sarah is now is putting together a longer-term Ethical Exit plan for herself that she'll be comfortable with financially, and will allow her control. *BAM! She's happier already!*

I could share dozens of stories like Sarah's, but those are only examples of how others have been able to change their circumstances and create better lives. The real test is finding out what your story will be – by exploring what you're willing to do to create your best life.

Let me know. I'd be glad to include your story in my next book if you like!

Chapter 3
Reality Check

During the time I was on a quest to bring more significance and purpose into my life, I still had responsibilities. I had a house, a daughter in college, car payments, school tuition, financial obligations, and a family to consider. I didn't have the option to be irresponsible with my choices.

My husband and I had spent the biggest part of the last two years caring for his aging parents. That task alone consumed much of our time, and required a level of commitment and responsibility we, as a couple, had never experienced. It was more consuming than raising children had ever been. It was a constant 24-7 job, and it was totally unavoidable. While his dad battled with the challenges of Alzheimer's, we could see the effect that it was having on his mom. We loved his parents dearly, and wanted so badly to do the very best for them, but that also meant there would be sacrifices. No family trips, because there was no one to look after my husband's parents if we went away together. If we were able to escape for a few days, our focus was still on making sure all the bases were covered and his parents' needs would still be met.

That time was especially hard on my husband, as he assumed the role of the primary caregiver for both of his parents. One of the consequences of that role was that his limited availability to work left us relying on my income for support as a major contributor to the family budget. That was a role I didn't mind, but it was also a catch-22 for us. Because of his responsibilities with his parents, and his limited work hours, the dependency on my income increased. That, in turn, meant that options for me to quit my job to help him were no longer available. I tried to allow for as much flexibility in my work schedule as possible with my current corporate job, but those options were limited as well.

Can you see the cycle here?

One of my non-negotiable items on my own self-coaching journey surrounded the fact that whatever decisions I made had to come from a place of responsibility, and being able to avoid significantly, negatively impacting my family. While my needs were, at times, selfish from the perspective of my work, they also were made with the realization that my family needed my time and presence with them as well as my income. The tug-a-war within my heart and soul was sometimes overwhelming.

YOUR RESPONSIBILITY
You're no different from me, in that you have responsibilities and priorities you feel obligated to maintain. Your responsibilities and priorities, as well as timing, are key to the whole process of creating an Ethical Exit to move on to a life that you love.

You can't let yourself get caught in the paradox of emotions that will so naturally occur as you go down the path of changing your life. You'll have emotions that will seem somewhat contradictory to each other: *I need to be responsible. I want to quit my job and the thought of leaving makes me happy... but also makes me sad. Money is not everything... but I have bills to pay. I am anxious about a new venture... but I am calm about my decisions. I am scared of the unknown... but I am excited to discover. I want to help out more... but I have to keep my job and my salary.* These are all very real emotions that may swirl around in your head and keep you up at night.

The thoughts and beliefs you create around those emotions will influence you and the actions you'll be willing to take. Responsibility and fear are at the center of all of these emotions. Not only do you experience fear around changes, there's fear that surfaces when you say, "I don't want to let anyone down by acting irresponsibly."

The reality of this paradox hit me like a ton of bricks the day I realized I'd let my family down by acting responsibly.

I was at the funeral home with my husband after the death of his mother. It had been only about a year since he lost his father, and now his mom had died following a short bout with cancer. We'd kept his father at home for the full duration of his battle with Alzheimer's, but his mother's illness, within such a short time afterwards, had taken a toll on my husband and his brother.

I remember standing at the funeral home as we greeted guests, and feeling an overwhelming sense of guilt. I felt guilty for not having being there for my husband, to help more or to take care of his mother. I'd recently been given the new work assignment that required me to spend the summer months in Florida. At the same time, my daughter was preparing to go to college, and in order for her to be able to spend any time with me over that summer, she'd have to join me in Florida. That was one of the most awkward family summers we've ever spent. My husband couldn't join us in Florida due to his mother's illness, and I couldn't go home due to the restrictions of my job.

My husband's mother died the day I moved my daughter to college. In that moment, I knew things had to change for me. My realization was that my commitment to being responsible with my job was the very thing that had caused me to act irresponsibly with the things that I consider to be my top priority. My family was the most important thing to me. Somehow, I'd have to trust there would be a way for me to honor my responsibilities.

RESPONSIBILITY RANKINGS

Clients come to me all the time with similar stories about feeling trapped in a cycle of perceived obligations and priorities. They seek me out to help them process the level of guilt and discontentment that accompany those feelings, which can be overwhelming.

In my coaching process I use an exercise to help them clarify their commitments by having them list and then rank all of their current responsibilities. I then ask them to describe or share with me some stories of times in which they feel that those responsibilities were dropped. When they begin telling the stories as to why responsibilities were overlooked, their reactions are very emotional. Clients list responsibilities such as home, family, children, parents, church, friends, bills, etc. When they finish and look at the list, they realized they'd let the ball drop on most of these already. The irony is that the number one reason they'd dropped the ball was due to other "responsible obligations."

If you want to start exploring your Responsibility Rankings, you can download, it along with other supportive information on my website at www.jeanneboschert.com/downloads. If you'd like me to guide you through any of these processes, please feel free to contact me or set up a time for us to talk.

WORKSHEET: RESPONSIBILITIES

COLUMN 1: List of all the personal areas that you feel are things that you are responsible for.

COLUMN 2: Think of a time when you have dropped the ball with that responsibility.

COLUMN 3: Write the reason that these were dropped.

What did you discover about your responsibilities? Have your responsibilities made you irresponsible? **Your coach will work with you to identify how these actions could be blocking our progress.**

I'll remember this example until I'm old and gray – a man who was the CEO of a large corporation. He was someone everyone looked up to, and he had a great professional reputation. He contacted me to coach him around some very specific issues going on with his team at work, and their performance. He related how he felt responsible for making the team run smoothly. I was very aware that the word "responsibility" was used quite frequently as he talked. He was very proud of his level of responsibility.

One day, the CEO mentioned that he needed to stray from our normal session and hoped that I didn't mind. I assured him that it was his session and he was free to be coached on anything he chose. He tried to assure me that he only needed me to hear him out on this and give him some friendly advice. He certainly didn't feel that he needed coaching about any personal matters! He went on to share with me how his relationship with his son was going through some challenges. He felt that his son was being unreasonable, and not understanding the CEO's responsibilities at work. I took him through some coaching thought-work and explorations of real circumstances, at which time the CEO began to cry. He had missed two of his son's baseball games in the last month because of his responsibilities. It was sad and also very real. My client's awareness of what he had *allowed his life to be reduced to* hit him blindside that day, as he processed the feelings that his need to be responsible on his job had caused for his son. Being responsible had actually made the CEO irresponsible!

How do we stop this madness? I'll share that with you after one more example.

I'm working with someone we'll call Elizabeth. Her husband has retired and is on a fixed income. Her children work, but they both have minimum wage positions, so she has traditionally found herself helping the children financially when they need it. Those situations usually involve grandchildren and extras. She has a home that is paid for and she currently brings in a six-figure income.

Elizabeth's biggest concerns are that she is an absent grandmother from her grandchildren's lives, and her husband has recently had health concerns that increase her desire to be more available for his care. She has a high stress job that delivers a high salary but little satisfaction. She has been in the industry for years, and has the respect of everyone as the expert in the field, but feels trapped and is dealing with a lack of passion and joy in her life. On almost every occasion we meet, she says about her life, "This is just not fun anymore."

Those close to Elizabeth are supportive of her to change roles; her only resistance was internal. Like many of us, she's had the overwhelming need to act responsibly. To create her ideal Ethical Exit, Elizabeth has designed and begun a plan in which she's started an online business with a partner in her spare time that will cushion her transition financially. We discussed that she now has two jobs, but since she had a great deal of flexibility in her full time role, and a partner in her online business, she was comfortable with managing her time equally to create and reach her long term goals.

It's been amazing to watch as Elizabeth did the work to take control of her life. She did it in such a way as to create a plan that she can feel passionate about, and at the same time fulfill her feelings of responsibility and commitment to her family. This will definitely be a temporary situation for her, because she's already engaged in her own Ethical Exit strategy.

I've shared these stories with you to let you know that real people are able to make responsible changes to their lives every day, and you can too. You can create your own best life that will include the exact ingredients you want. But to do that, you do have to get started. Reading about others doing it will not make it happen for you. You're in charge of what you want your life to be, so let's get started!

Chapter 4
Reading All The Signs

There were so many signs along the way, telling me that I needed to make changes in my life – not only for my emotional health, but my physical health as well. The signs were lighting up like a Los Angeles freeway. I was tired all the time and was having recurrent infections, due to my immune system being just stinking shot. I'd gained more than 30 pounds, and was unable or unwilling to expend the energy to eat or exercise properly. I found myself being snippy with my family and easily annoyed by my kids. My level of tolerance with my co-workers was diminishing, and my level of joy and engagement was waning too. While at work, I tried my best to do my best and give my best, but found it harder and harder to expend the energy that required. By the time I was ready to admit that things needed to change, I had a less than perfect attitude about myself. I wanted things to change, but did I really believe they could?

I'd been sent back to Florida for yet another week, my 24th week on the road, and I was exhausted, to say the least. The company had asked me to help consolidate and coordinate an office move. I was feeling the pressure of getting it all done perfectly and in a timely manner, and I felt that the site personnel was less than engaged in a process that they should have owned.

My boss and I communicated daily, and she was very supportive and aware of the problem. She let me know that not only was the team who'd been assigned to help with the move not going to be there, she'd totally miscommunicated with everyone involved in the move. Boxes had not been purchased, nothing had been packed, and yet the movers were due at 8 a.m.

I found myself having a key moment that day as I was cleaning out the office's refrigerator. For all of you who don't actually know me, I'd like to clarify that I didn't mind cleaning out the refrigerator! Any of you who've worked with me know that I don't find any job "beneath" me. I try to be a servant leader, and any job that needs to be done is my job. But, for some mysterious reason, that day with my head in the refrigerator and my butt in the air, I had a key moment! It was this: *I knew I was done.* I no longer felt that I was living a significant life.

What I felt was a clear sign that it was time to awaken my spirit to step up and show up in my own life. What I realized was that although I was being a servant leader and willing to do the job, the company could pay someone way less than my salary to clean out the refrigerator! I felt in some strange way that I was not being fair to the company, or honoring the skills I knew I was capable of providing. So it was time to honor my purpose.

One of my core beliefs – that I teach and lead with *now* – revolves around that moment. When I felt that I was no longer adding significant value to the company, I felt I owed it to my boss to leave. I was not showing up in the refrigerator as *the best me*.

HEEDING THE SIGNS

I don't want to give you unrealistic expectations about the days you'll face after you make the decision to change your life. The signs I got along the way were very important. The positive signs were very affirming, and I took the negative comments as caution signs, not stop signs, for my decisions going forward.

One of the very first signs of affirmation came from a lady I'd watched and admired for the past several months. She was my new boss. I remember vividly the day I entered my new boss's office to talk with her, after my "refrigerator awakening." I had typed out a resignation for her, as well as a thank-you note to the CEO of the company. The moment I sat down with her, we began to discuss my recent assignment, and I gave a brief overview of the challenges I had encountered and the solutions I'd implemented. She looked at me, and I began to tear up. She was very supportive and gracious as I gave my pre-leaving speech. I'll never forget that when I told her I needed to share some things with her, she said, "I already know why you're here. I knew this was going to happen." She went on to say, "I totally understand and I don't blame you. Frankly, I'm jealous." We joked then as we talked about my transition plan for a few minutes, and she hugged me before I left.

I've thought about that day many times. As I write about it today, I still find her words gracious and comforting, but more than anything else they were *affirming*. They were what I needed at that moment, that one soft voice that understood that my leaving had nothing to do with the company, but everything to do with my need for living a significant life.

Not every voice or piece of advice I got was quite that affirming. I heard everything from, "What are you thinking?" and, "What are you going to do all day?" to "Why would you do that? I thought you loved that job?" The truth of the matter was, I did love the job. I loved the people and what I was doing, for the most part, and that was part of the reason it was so hard to leave. It took me so long to listen to my own internal voice because I had a secure income, and I really did love my co-workers.

I felt a loss at the same time I felt a longing. If I'd hated the job and hated my boss, and if everyone around me had been a jerk, leaving would have been a no-brainer for me. But that was not the case.

WORKSHEET: EVERYBODY

This is for the thoughts that you think "everybody" has about you or your life, or for the comments that "everybody" is saying. List the comment in the space provided and next to every statement write at least 3-5 people that are proven to have said or are thinking those things. Your coach can work with you to challenge these beliefs and identify where they may be blocking you.

STATEMENT	PEOPLE

Were you able to get evidence to support your belief?

NAYSAYERS VERSUS CHEERLEADERS

As you make decisions in your life, and about your life, you'll encounter both naysayers and cheerleaders. It will be important to be able to take the mixed messages you'll receive and run them through the desire filter of your own heart.

There are lots of questions you can ask yourself around each of the people and comments that you'll hear. The answers will guide you in the direction of your very best conclusion.

Ask yourself if the person offering advice is someone whose opinion will matter in the long run. Is this someone who has your best interests at heart? Are they traditionally a risk-averse person? If so, you'll want to do more research on what they're sharing with you. Are they living their best and most productive life? If not, why would you want to listen to them? Are they someone you consider wise? Have they gone through a similar process? Another good question is one that life coach Martha Beck asks: "Are they living it to give it?"

The answers to these questions can be part of your guidance. Who the person is, and the role they play in your life, will determine the level of credibility you should attach to their feedback and advice. You can then decide if their advice is important enough that you want to take it, or if it's just a dream-robber you want to ignore. You have the option take advice or trash it!

Ben Ament, in his book *The Dream Year*, gives us these comforting words to help us deal with the various naysayers we encounter: "Don't be surprised if other people do not fully embrace your dream or even understand it right away. Skepticism and doubt are welcome barriers that keep other people from doing what you do. When they fail to understand what you're doing, consider it a gift. You have a dream that only you can see." He goes on to explain that: "One day people will come to embrace what you see. But until then, consider your isolation a safety laboratory to work out the kinks in your dream – to and try and fail without the scrutiny of others."

WORKSHEET: NAYSAYERS VS CHEERLEADERS

On the right list all the Naysayers, take note of the negative or concerning comments that they have made. On the left list all of the cheerleaders and supporters that have given you positive or affirming comments.

Take a look at each statement and see if those are factual or feeling comments and discuss each one with your coach to dissolve beliefs that will not support your attaining your goals.

TAKE IT OR TRASH IT

I use the Take It or Trash It exercise in my workshops to dissolve some of the beliefs my clients have around comments from the people in their lives.

First, I have them list all the tidbits and words of wisdom they've received about their new, adventurous life. As they go through this process, I try to observe their reactions – to get insight as to the impact and influence they've allowed others to have in their lives. I then have them utilize the questions I mentioned above, to filter the credibility of the feedback. If your spouse has an opinion, it's generally going to be filtered with a different level of credibility than the lady who does your nails!

When you do this exercise, it's usually pretty clear by the end which comments you should take as feedback, and which you should trash as invalid opinions.

Something you can do to help put things into perspective, and recognize your irrational thoughts, is when you catch yourself saying "everybody says this" or "everybody thinks that." Ask yourself for proof. When my clients say things like this, I ask them to tell me the names of "everybody." When they're faced with the reality of their thoughts, they usually begin to laugh, both at themselves and at the fact that they now realize how silly those statements and beliefs have been.

If you want to know if you should Trash it or Take It and want to identify your cheerleaders, you can download worksheets I've created to help you do that at my website, www.jeanneboschert.com/downloads.

WORKSHEET: TAKE IT OR TRASH IT

Take a look at the previous exercise and write the comments of each person you listed. Look at each person and the statement to assign a level of importance to the comment, 3 being the most important and 1 being the least. If the comment came from your most significant other it would be graded with a 3, if it came from a casual acquaintance then the weight would be lower on the scale toward a 1. Your coach will work with you to identify how these thoughts could be blocking our progress.

	RATING

I encourage you not to be disheartened by the voices of naysayers. Consider yourself in great company. Walt Disney had them. Orville and Wilber Wright had them. Bill Gates had them. Thomas Edison, Mother Teresa, and even Jesus had them. The list could go on forever. Don't worry if other people don't understand or don't see your dream. It's your life and your dream and it was given to you for a reason. It's not theirs.

Naysayers and cheerleaders will exist all along your path. They're external signs that you'll encounter. There will be many other external signs you can recognize along this journey and it will be important that you don't get deterred or blocked by them. Look at each challenge as a new tool to add to your tool belt. Each one will strengthen you and help build your character. You'll learn new ways of doing things and as you do you'll have more tools to help you build your perfect life.

PAY ATTENTION
I've seen many great people with really great plans throw in the towel the minute they encounter the first hurdle in the road. If you're

going to create something as big and wonderful as your ideal life, then understand that hurdles will exist. The best way to deal with these hurdles is to examine them closely, see why they're there, and determine what you can learn from them.

Many times hurdles are present for a reason. They may be about timing, they may be a detour from an even more difficult path, or they could be there to help you find out how high you're willing to jump for your dreams. You're not meant to always ignore them, which could cause you to fall. You can't always resist them and just stop because they're there. You're meant to acknowledge their presence and determine why they're there. They may be there to direct you to a greater and more amazing path.

INTERNAL SIGNS

You may have already noticed some internal signs that you feel are leading you to a path that's better for you. Acknowledge that you may have missed some of those signs along the way. Don't beat yourself up about it. You may have found yourself, like many of us, just going through the motions of life. It's at those times that there may have been signs in the path, but we didn't see or understand their significance.

My body and my health were some of the signs that I ignored and missed.

I encourage you to pay attention to your body. It knows you and can act as a regulator for you, if you're willing to listen. How many times have you felt that something just wasn't right? You didn't know what it was, but you had a feeling in the pit of your stomach that something was off. It could have been about a person you didn't feel could be trusted, or that you were possibly not being as cautious as you needed to be in a business deal, or that you should wait on a particular decision. These instincts and intuitive responses are built into the DNA of each of us for a reason. The ability to sense danger was essential in the survival of early man, and it is essential to our best life today. Some people have a stronger sense of intuition than others because they've been keenly sensitive to it and given it attention. Intuition is an important tool and you should pay attention to the direction in which it leads you.

As a nurse, I'm very familiar with the physical responses our bodies have to what we offer it, in the same way our emotional and intuitive responses react to what we perceive in each situation. The gift our body gives back is a direct result of the gift we offered to our bodies. If we give it high, prolonged stress, it gives us high blood pressure and heart disease. If we serve up bad eating habits and poor exercise, it gives us an overweight and weak body. If we allow excessive prolonged worry in our lives, we can end up with ulcers and depression.

I ask you to pay attention and give valid thought to what your body is telling you. One simple example of how your body may be sending you messages is that if you're feeling constantly tired and overwhelmed, your body may be begging you to slow down. If we fail to listen, often the result is that we become sick or catch a bug of some kind that will force us to slow down.

I share this information with you because as you go on this journey to make changes in your life, there will be stress and worry and anxious moments. There will be many changes going on as you create your best life or work to create your Ethical Exit. Each of these changes will require that you're paying attention to your emotional and physical signs and are making time for self-care. These signs can be beneficial to being able to live and enjoy your final results.

Allow me to share with you a time in my life during which signs and hurdles could have been easily misinterpreted if I hadn't had a commitment to the greater cause and purpose.

My husband and I started a company in 1999 that was a totally new venture. We were both in healthcare careers, and an opportunity presented itself. We decided to open our own practice. We did all the prep work, made the best hiring decisions we could, and put our blood sweat and tears into that startup. It was a company that would require that we contract with a managed care agency. The state where we lived hired a managed care company to come in and take over programs they had traditionally been overseeing. We followed all the regulations, completed all the training, and secured the contract that the state required of us. We put our savings on the line and were off and running.

Ninety days into the business, the state decided they would pull the contract from the management company, and private practices would no longer be eligible to participate. It was a pivotal moment. We had put everything we had into that business and quit our jobs and had no other options. We could either take this as a sign that the universe didn't want us to play in this arena, or we could do something. I chose to not see this as a stop sign, but as a hurdle to strengthen me for a greater purpose. It was my mission to do something.

I went to work quickly and rallied other providers throughout the state. We organized a strategy and went to the capital. I felt strongly enough that what we were doing was right and, after all, I didn't have anything else to lose. I was naïve enough to believe that if I could just talk to the right people, and share what was happening in the lives of these patients, they would see that this decision was wrong. I'm happy to say that after three months of deliberations with the state's Department of Human Services, and many legislative sessions –

where I had to tell my story to senators and representatives and advocate for what I knew in my heart was the right path – we won! That's right, we beat the so-called system, and were able to change laws and make a difference. We got rid of a single option, state-run system, and opened the network for patients to be in charge of their care and choose who they wanted as their provider for health services.

Was that a *big* hurdle? You bet it was, but the results were even bigger. Many times, the size of the hurdle can be proportionate to the end results.

That was 15 years ago. I often wonder what would have happened if I had looked at the size of the external sign, and seen the enormous uphill battle it would likely be, and decided to throw in the towel. As I write this, I get passionate all over again and feel my heartbeat racing as I share. It was important for me to share this story to let you know that there are times when things in our paths seem impossible. But those things are placed in our paths as tests of our determination and commitment to doing the right thing, and working to create that life of significance for ourselves.

It will be that same passion for doing the right thing for your life that you'll need when those moments occur – moments that will be meant to test you and not trip you, moments that are meant to see if you have what it takes to make it to your goal. Those will be the moments of significance that you'll long to create in your life over and over again. Don't fail the test. Don't throw in the towel too soon. Watch for signs. Pay attention to your body. What is it telling you? Remember that for many of you, this feeling of significance is what's leading you down this path to live your most productive life.

Chapter 5
Yes You Can! But Should You?

There was a point in my drive to create my ideal life when it could have gone a totally different way. I've already shared with you that I loved my job, my boss, my company and my paycheck. I was struggling with the internal desire to leave versus the love for the company where I worked.

One day, I was looking through my email, as I seemed to be doing continuously, when I ran across what I thought was the most awesome internal job posting I could imagine. I felt like that God had answered my prayer and this was going to be the "fix" for all that was going on with me.

I had already done my wish list for my new life, and when I reviewed this position, I saw that it met every criteria I wanted and needed for my new, purposeful life. I would be home every night, I would get to stay with the company I loved, I could maintain my work friends, I would get to reconnect with friends within my local work community, I would have continued flexibility with my schedule, and the universe would shine on me!

I immediately picked up the phone and called my friend who was handling the recruiting for the job, to inquire about next steps. I then went straight home and sent in my updated resume and then I waited for the call. The call didn't come right away, but I was patient. After all, I was just sure this was my answer. I let my boss know that I had submitted for the position and, as always, she was supportive and encouraging, as she knew how much I missed my family. She even told me that she had talked to the supervisor of the division where the new position was, and given me a good recommendation.

I was called in for an interview, and felt anxious going in. I was interviewing with someone who was very new with the company, and I was not sure if they even knew my name before I'd applied for the new position. My second interview for the position was someone I'd worked with and I felt comfortable that it would be favorable.

That day, when I left the first interview, I can honestly say that I had a gut feeling that something didn't go right. The second interview was awesome. The interviewer even said to me, "This seems like a no-brainer," and was excited that I'd wanted to consider taking the position.

There was nothing I could put my finger on about that first interview. I was having one of those gut feelings that we just talked about. There was no big blunder or stumble. It was one of those situations where I could tell that, for some reason, my first interviewer was not that into me. She had been very nice and professional, but I still felt that vague, intuitive sign. I tried to remain optimistic, but the call did not come. I finally worked up the courage to call my friend in recruiting. I needed to get some closure about my vague optimism. When she answered the call, I knew I hadn't made it. She really didn't want to disappoint me. She knew how badly I wanted that position.

"Jeanne," she said, "they really want to hire someone with more recent hospital experience. I am so sorry." Those were hard words for me hear and probably for her to say. I felt bad for her. I had really thought this was going to be my answer, *and it was*, but not in the way I first thought it would be.

The signs were adding up. It was time for me to create my life and go outside the comfort zone I'd known for more than seven years. It was time to create an Ethical Exit and then create the life of my dreams.

I was not angry or blaming. For me, there was an overwhelming sense of affirmation that my ideal life was not going to exist in my comfort zone. I would have to leave what was safe and comfortable in order to know what was great and amazing. I would have to create an Ethical Exit before I could create the life of my dreams.

I can honestly say that if I had been offered that job, I would not be here. I would not be writing this book, and I would not have the life of freedom and adventure that I currently get to experience. I would have been comfortable to remain in the confines of the job that met all of my criteria. But there was a bigger plan, and I needed to learn to trust it to unfold.

HEAD VERSUS HEART DECISIONS

I've learned so much in my career about decisions and commitments. One of the things I see my clients get caught up in is the trap of confusion between the two. I see it all the time. People make a decision, and then change their mind when the next shiny object comes along. Decisions are made by the intellectual part of us that constantly evolves and grows and learns. As new information comes in, new decisions will be formed around the new information.

It's going to be very important as you go forward to continue to ask yourself this question: "Is this a decision or is this a commitment?" Is your decision to make an Ethical Exit, or make transformational changes in your life, only an intellectual *decision* that can change tomorrow, or is it a *commitment* that you will make that will redefine your life?

I've come to understand that commitments are very different from decisions. Commitments are made from a much deeper place. They're made at an emotional and heart level. Commitments are easier to be grounded in because the level at which we're willing to go for them is deeper.

Decisions are very different from commitments. We decide lots of things every day: what we're going to wear, what we'll eat, how we'll work. Head decisions are often made on autopilot. Commitments don't change quickly or on a whim. For example, I'm committed to my family, I'm committed to my marriage, I'm committed to truth, I'm committed to learning. These are not beliefs that change on the fly, and it usually takes a great deal of additional information to cause such commitments to shift. They're not easily influenced based on circumstances.

Decisions are made with our heads and commitments are made from our hearts. I really want you to spend some time determining where your decisions are coming from. The difference between the two will definitely impact how you proceed. You may want to ask yourself, "From what level do my decisions around creating an Ethical Exit or designing my very best life come?"

SHOULD I STAY OR GO?

I work with clients all the time who waffle in the area of decisions and commitments. Many times, that's what leads them to me – they want help sorting out the difference and clarifying their confusion. One of the processes I use involves not only classifying their commitments, but helping them identify small changes that can be made or added to create their best life. If there are changes that can occur that will meet all of the items that they've listed on their Longing List, it can be possible to have their best life without making any exit at all.

It is totally possible to create your life in a way that will provide you with passion and joy and that can be done in any job market. I've seen some of the most joyful and committed people in minimum wage and hourly positions. What is ideal for you may not be ideal for me. Everybody deserves to live their very best life, no matter the occupation. The world needs every profession, and we need people who are committed and dedicated to that profession. When I hire a plumber, I want a committed plumber; when I hire a surgeon I want a committed surgeon; and when I go to Starbucks, I want to get a happy and joyful barista.

This is not always about starting your own company, or designing an off-the-wall business you know nothing about. Making slight changes in your current position could allow you to ethically exit the life that currently challenges you, and create a life you can love and be totally committed to execute.

IMPROVING THE SITUATION

I had a client I'll call Jonathan. He was a successful physician with a private practice and a wife and two great kids. He was respected in his community, involved in everything the kids did, and had an amazing home in the very best neighborhood. His wife didn't work outside the home. She was one of the best carpooling, stay-at-home, baseball moms in town. Jonathan's family was active in their church and in the local civic community. By most standards, they had the ideal life. I was surprised when Jonathan contacted me and asked for my service. What could possibly be wrong?

As we did the intake session and as I reviewed his homework, I was surprised by some of his answers. He proceeded to tell me he hated his job. I reminded him that he was a physician and had spent years educating himself for this path. We discussed the idea that he had what most people would refer to as a career, and not just a job. He told me he was considering closing his practice.

Over the next few weeks, I went on a coaching excavation with Jonathan to clarify the real source of his dissatisfaction and lack of fulfillment. He struggled with the realization that closing his practice as an emotional, knee-jerk decision could result in him losing everything: his wife, his home, his practice, and his self-respect.

We worked diligently, and Jonathan uncovered the realization that over the years, as he'd added responsibilities to his life, he'd let go of the things he loved and taken on tasks he hated. Prior to having a practice and children, Jonathan had been an avid big game hunter. When he talked about the thrill of the hunt, he visibly physically changed. His eyes brightened, his voice became excited and passionate, and he became obviously energized.

As we continued to discuss the areas of his life and practice that he felt were overwhelming to him, I took notes. His one area of negative reactions came when he discussed having to handle personnel issues within his office. Prior to having children, his wife had managed the day-to-day functions in the office, including the hiring and firing and corrective actions around office staff. This had worked very well for them.

As we progressed in our sessions, Jonathan agreed to look at adding back to his life those things which made him happy and finding someone to handle the personnel issues at the office. It was obvious that his joy had not been taken from him; he had given it away without even realizing it.

I'm happy to say that Jonathan still has a thriving practice. His oldest child is now in college, and goes with his dad on big game hunts at least twice a year. Jonathan hired an office manager to handle the personnel details and drama in the office, and he created a life both personally and professionally that he now loves. His Ethical Exit involved staying in his business, but creating an exit plan around his personal pleasure, and for business-based emotional peace.

Chapter 6
Planning to Leave

Earlier in the book, I shared what I was going through on the day I resigned my position with my last company. It's important to me that I share with you the level of responsibility I felt not only to myself, but also to my employer, until my very last day. As I went through my responsibility lists, it was important to me that I not forget my responsibility to the job and the company I was leaving. I wanted to work with the same level of integrity and give my best until my very last day at that company.

After I resigned, and cried with many of the people I'd spent and shared life with for more than seven years, I wanted to make sure I honored what the company would need from me to ease the transition. I tried to ensure that I communicated my actions daily with my boss so she'd be aware of the steps I took, and the leaving process could continue without interruption. I continued to interview new employees up until two days before I left. I could, with honesty and integrity, talk to them about what a great company it was. I made sure I didn't disrupt the sites I was working with by discussing my leaving with them prior to the announcement of the transition plan. I made sure all my peers knew how to reach me even after my 30-day notice, in case they needed any additional information from me.

I've seen way too many cases of people resigning a job, and then going in to work before their time is up, as if someone had done an injustice to them. They stopped giving their best a long time before they left, and were only showing up for the paycheck. That is not, in my southern social way of being, the right thing to do. I would not be a person of integrity if I decided to ride out a notice or give any less that my best for that last month.

When I titled this book *The Ethical Exit*, it was about more than the last day of work. It was also with the intention that I could instill in the mind of anyone thinking about leaving that they should do so with the good of all parties involved. Plan well for yourself, but plan well for your company, too. I've witnessed some pretty messy exits in my career, and there is never a winner in those cases. The company suffers as does the employee who's leaving.

I encourage any of you thinking of leaving your position to do your best to exit with integrity. If you're trying to create your very best life, leaving your job in an unethical way may not be the best way to start. *Take this job and shove it* doesn't really qualify as an Ethical Exit.

EXECUTION IS EVERYTHING

Now that you've come to the decision that you're willing to do the work, create the plan, and make the commitment to create the life you love, you won't be sorry. Your journey will begin with you creating an Ethical Exit plan, because creating that Ethical Exit is only the beginning.

The exit marks a big step in creating a life you love and are passionate about. Once you exit, or maybe even prior to your exit, the work will begin. Execution of the plan you've wrestled with and dreamed of is about to be set in motion.

The pace at which you execute your plan will determine the speed at which you're able to create and live the life that you love. There will be challenges you will not have anticipated, even with the best of plans. So get ready for them. Don't think this is going to be a cakewalk. Once you're content and clear with your plan and your ability to carry it out responsibly, it will be up to you to execute it and add the ingredients to your life plan to make it happen. There will be dates to set for your leaving, timelines for executing your new plan, deadlines that you'll need to establish, as well as a new definition of normal. Plan this phase like you did your corporate strategy but this plan is your life strategy. Now is the time to tap into your corporate killer mode and create the structure around your plans to make them happen.

I'll share with you one of the unforeseen challenges that hit me blindside. It was trying to create the new normal for me. I had a plan for a website, and a well-defined design. I hired one of the most highly recommended webmasters for my industry, and thought I had all the bases covered. One component that took me by surprise was that of timing. I'd left my position in September, and had planned to give myself until January to launch my new business. I'd thought three months would be plenty of time, given all the preparation I'd done, but there were a couple of factors I hadn't considered: my designer was taking off for several weeks around the holidays, and the programmer I was paying for with my new back-end program to create launch campaigns was due to be a daddy any day! Surprise! My plans just got pushed back more than 30 days.

This was not planned, but it was also not catastrophic. As an independent business owner, I no longer had an IT department available at the touch of a button who could fix it. I also didn't have a big marketing and education department to be my go-to for resourcing, and I was quickly learning that even though I could do many of the daily business tasks, the time that took was preventing me from creating the programs and business platforms I needed for my launch. I realized that I needed to execute a different plan.

It was at this point that I contacted and hired a virtual assistant to help me. She was also familiar with WordPress, and was able to help me get clear on how to work on my website while my designer was off on holiday leave. As an added bonus, she was also familiar with the program for running my online campaign, and was able to finish my launch materials.

Execution – and flexibility in execution – will be important for you to master in your new role as the CEO of your own life.

PRIORITIES

An exercise I've used when training groups of nurses involves being able to determine when there's a problem, and the priority of that problem. I asked the nurses to prioritize and distinguish the urgent tasks from the everyday tasks.

This same exercise of prioritizing will be useful to you when you become the master of your own schedule, as it will be important for you to be able to prioritize your work.

There are tasks you'll label as urgent, and there will be delayed tasks. You'll need to look at each one and make a decision: which tasks do you need to handle yourself, which can be delegated to someone else, and which are tasks you can put off and get done only as free time arises. As a person who is now in charge of her own time and tasks, I encourage you to make this a part of your everyday routine as you go about planning to create and design your best life. Learning to prioritize will be a key ability when it comes to executing your plans.

WORKSHEET: PRIORITIES

As you make plans to create your ideal life, make a list of all the elements and tasks that you feel will need to be completed. See if there are steps within each task that have to be done in order to finish the task. Then prioritize each task into the category of urgent or every day. Once you are able to decide the urgent tasks it will be important to work with your coach to define the timeframes and steps that will be required to complete each one.

TASKS

URGENT	**EVERY DAY**

I have a client I'll refer to as Connie. She was an accomplished employee at a hospital, recently promoted to a position she readily admitted she didn't want. Departments consolidated and she was chosen to lead the new division. Connie was well-respected, highly intelligent, and totally miserable. She found herself disengaging, not wanting to be at work, and she no longer considered her job a dream job, as she once had. The company had made changes, and Connie found herself questioning some of the leadership decisions and no longer respecting the decisions of her superiors.

As we talked, it became clear that Connie wasn't willing to stay in her current position. She'd probably stayed past the point of discontentment, and was entering the point of disdain. In our conversations over the next months, she experienced challenges with emotional waffling, naysayers versus cheerleaders, and obstacles that could have been seen as reasons to throw in the towel and abandon her plan, but she didn't. She continued the course and created a life that now offers her everything she wanted that was part of her core values. Connie has freedom, as she does contract work with a partner, and she has time for travel and connecting with friends again. She's redone part of her home, and is planning a trip abroad. Connie is truly living a life she's passionate about, and that brings her joy and a sense of fulfillment.

The process I helped Connie to walk through is the same process available to you. You can choose to create your best life too!

Chapter 7
When The Exit Is Not Your Idea

What if you're in a situation that's not ideal, in that you haven't been able to choose your own work fate? What then?

You just got invited to your boss's office. Wow! What could this be about? Maybe they've noticed all the hard work and time you've put into this company. Finally!

Wrong!

They've noticed all right. They've invited you to your home away from home to free up your future by letting you go. You're shocked... or maybe not. You may have seen it coming. After all, they've been talking about downsizing, and you've seen the financials. You knew they were going to have to make some adjustments, but you were hoping and praying you'd get a pass.

This is only one of the multitude of scenarios that can occur when you're given the invitation to put your belongings in a box and say your good-byes, because your career at this job is over.

What do you do at this point? How do you react in the right way when you feel that something went wrong? That's a question I'm asked over and over and over.

In the past few years, I've done consulting within the healthcare industry. This is an industry that's going through a huge systemic overhaul. Companies are still trying to balance their new work shift to know how to play in the new way of providing healthcare services. That being said, with all the changes have come cuts and closings and mergers and layoffs. It's become a very familiar scenario.

Such changes are not isolated to healthcare. These scenarios exist in every industry, and in Every Town, U.S.A. Things change, and industries work very hard to find new and more efficient ways to do business. The corporate world in today's market is evolving in many, many ways. Technology has afforded new opportunities and, at the same time, decreased the need for personnel. It's not uncommon to be competing with a variety of very talented candidates when a position becomes available. It's also not uncommon that when people are let go, those positions are not being refilled, because the work of the person who was let go is being shifted and allocated to others who are already in place. These measures are usually implemented to cut costs and increase margins; this is not traditionally a personal vendetta! Regardless of how being laid off may feel, it is just a different or better or more efficient way for the business to change the way it operates.

As these shifts within the workplace happen, I've observed two distinct effects. One is obviously the loss of manpower, but the second effect is the burnout of those who remain. As employees are asked to do more with less, the level of disengagement and burnout has increased. If this is happening to you that may be part of the reason you've been drawn to this writing.

Even in the most difficult circumstances, there are ways you can still create an Ethical Exit. Any situation can be handled with integrity and professionalism. When you respond in this way, it can elevate your pride in yourself and leave your supervisors surprised. Reactions that are calm, and exiting employees who appear to see both sides of the situation open the option to receive a possible reference. There's still the option to say to your employer, "Thank you for the opportunity to have worked here." You can express to them the positive things you've learned while you were there, as well as acknowledging any relationships you made. You can respond to the circumstances with a level of tact and respect that will leave no doubt that you're making an Ethical Exit, despite the circumstances.

TOTALLY PERFECT

I try to help people to see that there are hidden gems even in these situations. If an unexpected exit is happening to you, I suggest you start by listing all the things that are totally perfect about what has just happened. Only focus on what's perfect about this. When I've done this with my clients, I've heard answers like these: "I was really run down, so now I can pay attention and get some rest." "I can go see my grandchildren." "I can help my husband more at home." "I get to do some volunteer work I've not had time for." "I get to reconnect and go to lunch with some friends." "I finally get to paint my living room."

You can see pretty quickly how changing the thought, and looking at the totally perfect elements of a bad situation, can be freeing. It can also seed positive thoughts within you, so that you can set intention to make those things happen.

Unfortunately, when something such as the loss of a job occurs, most people go into a state of panic and worry that unfortunately keeps them stuck. Because of the catastrophe that is created within the mind, it paralyzes positive actions. This can create a downward spiral of thought that leaves us believing we'll be alone, homeless, and living under a bridge.

WORKSHEET: TOTALY PERFECT

We all have challenging and difficult situations in our lives. It is important for us to be able to make the best decisions that we put each situation in the best perspective. In order to do that we need to realize that there can be great things that are available to us even in the most difficult circumstances. I want you to take a look at the difficult situation that you are currently working on and to list everything that is totally perfect about this situation. Be sure to share your insights wit your coach.

_____

_____

_____

_____

_____

_____

_____

_____

_____

ANALYSIS OR PARALYSIS

Terminations, layoffs, and firings are all events that can be traumatic, but they can also be opportunities. I'll share with you two conversations I've had in the last three months with people who've been given an exit that was not their idea.

The first conversation was with a woman I'll call Maria, a single mother of two, who has spent the majority of her career immersed in the community of her career. Her friends were at work, her connections were through work, and so were her identity and self-worth. She was at the top of her game... or so she thought, because she had a long-standing relationship with the owner of the company and he was very secure with her work ethics. While that was important, it was not something that was shared when new owners entered the picture.

As Maria continued to work, and take great pride in her ability to maintain teams and a great company reputation, her new and very strong female boss was *not* her fan. Maria identified signs along the way, but she never thought they would result in the loss of her job.

For Maria, the invitation to go to the office and the subsequent future freedom conversation was very difficult. She had never given any thought as to what her life would be like without that job in that industry. With her severance and the non-compete timeframe drawing near, I asked Maria, "What do you want to do?" After almost six months, the answer for her is still unclear and under review. Her fears, and the loss of her job, have left her feeling unsure of her move. She's taking her time to figure things out.

The second story I'll share is also about a single mom with two children, who I'll call Janet. Janet was totally caught off guard when she was asked to do a conference call to discuss some potential concerns. It was that call in which she was also given the future freedom conversation. She was informed that her final day would be immediate.

Unlike Maria, Janet was not offered a severance, and she had no non-compete. She'd been working for the company for several years, and had worked most of that time in a travel position. She'd recently become tired of the travel and her children were beginning to make comments that left her feeling the guilt of her commitment. Decisions were being made at the company that Janet felt were not in the best interest of the company, and she knew she'd become disillusioned with the way things were going.

When we spoke, Janet had been let go on Friday, and she'd already set up interviews for the following week. I asked her to step away from the situation and consider the gift she'd been given. She'd been very unhappy, had hated being away from her children, and her relationships had suffered. She was able to see the positive opportunity she now had, to find out what will be the best for her future and her family.

Since then, Janet has explored a business opportunity she's planning to develop, and is now very busy making the contacts and doing the work to make it happen. She'll get the life she wants and it will be so much better than the one she had because she has the mindset and intention to make it happen.

Those are just two examples. They could be you or someone you know. Maria and Janet's real stories of success will be revealed as they both continue to make progress and create their new glorious path in life. They will both get what they want, but it will be at their own pace, based on their ability to get clear on their goals, set the intentions, define their strategy and execute their plans.

You can see that those two scenarios are similar but had very different effects on those involved. The difference in any situation is in the thoughts we create for ourselves about the situation.

In the work of Byron Katie, she use a very simple questioning technique to confirm or dissolve the thoughts we've assigned to any situation. The first thing to ask of any negative thought is to determine if it is true. Is it always true? Is there a time when it wasn't true? The next step is to explore how that thought serves you and what or who you would be without that thought. If you're able to self-coach around these questions, you are exceptional, but in many cases, this process is not something you can do alone. If you are having trouble getting through the hard thought work, you may need a coach who can walk the rocky path with you to get you to the other side to see the situation differently.

TURTLE STEPS – GETTING TO THE BEAUTY
Several years ago, I was on a cruise to Hawaii with family and friends. We'd gone to a wonderful place called Turtle Bay, to spend the day swimming with turtles and snorkeling in the cove. We'd been told of the beauty of the coral and the colorful fish in that bay and were looking forward to the adventure.

As we worked our way into the deeper areas off the shore, we noticed that one friend lagged behind. We continued on, very aware of the presence of a rocky coral reef as we tried to navigate without disturbing the swimming turtles. As I was determined to get to the deeper area where all the beautiful fish were, I was unaware of anything that would distract me from experiencing the beauty of the cove and the gorgeous fish. It was then that I realized that my friend had stopped. She was sitting on the rocks, paralyzed by the work it was taking to get to the beauty.

I went back to her with my other girlfriend, because I did not want to let my friend stay on the shore when I had seen the beauty that was a just on the other side of the difficult. It was the view of a lifetime. As I swam back for her, some in the group said to leave her alone and if she wanted to come, she would. Don't push her, they said, she can decide for herself. But what I could see that they could not was that my friend wanted to come and see. Everything in her wanted to see what I had seen, but she was paralyzed by the fear of the possible pain. She was unable at that moment to see how to get to the other side.

Her thoughts could have kept her on the bank for the rest of the day. Except for the fact that she was with me, the pushy people-reader who's never had a problem barging into someone's life. I coached, reached out, encouraged, cheered and gave a hand to help her through the rocky coral so she could make it to the other side. It was totally worth it.

My coaching style is much like my snorkeling style. I challenge my clients comfort with staying on the shore, especially since I've already seen the beauty on the other side of the difficult.

Come on in! The water's great!

Chapter 8
Inaction Can Be Your Enemy

Ok. You've made it past the point of decision, you've created a plan, and you've defined your Ethical Exit strategy. Now what? Well I'm going to share with you not only what I see for you, but what I did for myself to prevent my decent into what I refer to as The Valley of Do Nothing.

I belong to several groups that my industry refers to as Masterminds. Being in a Mastermind group usually involves weekly accountability calls, along with action steps, homework, and projects to do to help keep independent business owners on track. The intent of these groups is not only to promote accountability, but also for the sharing of resources that can be very helpful in an industry where people are sometimes solo business owners.

For instance, in one of my Mastermind groups, there are people who are experts in the social media world. This is very helpful, because we can call on them for help and support or hire them to implement in each of their areas of expertise if needed. A Mastermind group is definitely a healthy pool of contacts to help with business functions and tasks that seem unclear.

One thing that has also become clear to me in some of these groups is that there are people who have been unable to move forward. They've built a home in The Valley of Do Nothing. They're still stuck on things as simple as business card design, setting up a website, or developing a Facebook business page. They declare that they want to move their business forward and have an online presence, but have not taken any of the actions necessary in order for that to happen. I sometimes wonder if they think a website is set up by osmosis or something. It does not work that way.

I see people over and over who are paralyzed by their inability to take action. They will take up a large amount of time on the calls at times, complaining because their business is not growing. I have, on occasion, lovingly challenged the individual and offered to coach them to get started – only to sit in silence and not have the phone ring for help. Inaction is their enemy. I am not sure what they are afraid of, they have made all of the hard calls up to this point. They have a plan and have quit their jobs but now have no clue what to do next.

I warn you, if you find yourself going to visit in the Valley of Do Nothing, don't stay long or the next thing you know, you will have built yourself a comfortable home there. Determining your wants and your needs can help you get through this impasse and take action.

WHAT I WANT – WHAT I NEED
I recently was doing an activity with a client, titled "What I Want - What I Need." That is very simple but helps to get people moving because they get very clear picture.

Determine your Wants and Needs with a handy worksheet you can download at www.jeanneboschert.com.

It is very simple: I would have you write on a sheet of paper, divided down the middle. On the left you would write what you want, and on the right what you need in order to get that. You would be surprised how hard this exercise can be for some people.

If you have items on your want side, then there are things that you will need to do in order to get them. For example, if you want a website, you will need a designer, copy, logo, titles, how many pages, and e-commerce. These things don't just happen.

I had someone have a whole list of 23 things that they wanted, but could only share 3 things on the side what do they need in order to get those wants. Part of being able to move forward in your life and business is being able to identify both needs and wants.

When you are setting up a business for the very first time, these can be confusing and you sometimes don't know what you don't know. That is part of why when I designed my program, to help people to create the ethical exit and design the life they love. A large portion of that program involves helping clients to identify all of the components and pieces that they will need in order to run their particular type of business and create their new life.

WORKSHEET: WANTS VS NEEDS

You have a goals that you want to accomplish in your life. Please list the life goals that you have in the column on the left. Then in the right column write all the things that you will need in order to reach that particular goal. Consider this your quickstart guide for your ideal life. You coach can then help you get really clear about how, when and where you should start. Good luck at creating you plan and if you are feeling stuck anywhere along the way please contact your coach for assistance.

GOALS	NEEDED TO COMPLETE

IT'S ALL ABOUT YOUR BASE

Well, we have all heard the catchy tune that says, "It is all about the base, bout the base, bout the base" and I want to say to you yes it is! But in a much different way. As you begin to create the life of your dreams, you need to see it as building a literal structure, a base.

As a basic principle of physics and body mechanics, I learned the width of your base of support is directly proportional to the strength and height of your structure. So if you are wanting to build a great big life for yourself that reaches really high goals and potential, then you are going to need to secure for yourself a really wide and stable base of support.

Let's talk about the different types of supports that you will need to create and live your very best life.

BUSINESS SUPPORTS

Let's first discuss your business base of support. It is going to need to come in a variety of forms and with a variety of skills. You will need to develop a support system for your business that can deliver resources and connections that you may not need initially but as you grow and build your new life will need to be used.

If you are going to be starting a business, or looking at business opportunities in your newly created life, you will need legal, financial and business set up advice. You may need supports related to marketing, branding, advertising and social media development and management. You may want to work with a coach who can help connect you to the right resources and team members that you will need depending on the type of business that you will be establishing.

COACHING SUPPORTS

Secondly, you will need to establish a good base of accountability that will be separate from your emotional support network.

This accountability structure, for me, was that I had to have a coach who I knew had done what I was wanting to do. They had to have established credibility within my network, and it had to be someone that I felt that I could trust to help me get to the best solutions without any hidden agendas.

I've created a How to Find the Right Coach Checklist which I use when I'm finding support. I think it will help you too. You can download that at www.jeanneboschert.com/downloads.

My coach could not be someone that was in my emotional cheerleader network, although they are my biggest cheerleader. I needed for them to be able to give me feedback in order to get me going and keep me headed in the right direction. My coach was my accountability cheerleader.

There are a variety of coaching options available to meet every need. There are coaching packages, coaching groups, individual coaching or VIP yearlong programs. It will be important as you look for your coach that you explore the options that will best suit your unique goals.

WORKSHEET: HOW TO FIND THE RIGHT COACH

Read through the list and check the appropriate box for each statement.

		YES	NO
1.	Am I comfortable with their style?		
2.	Has the coach done what I want to do?		
3.	Does the coach have relatable experience in both life and business?		
4.	Do I feel that I can trust this coach?		
5.	Are they easy to talk to?		
6.	Are they able to offer options in their coaching that meet my timeframe?		
7.	Are they willing to support me through the process?		
8.	Will I have a way to communicate with them outside of our calls?		
9.	Is there the option to have intensive work if I need it?		
10.	Does the coach have additional resources that they can recommend?		
11.	Is the coach credible?		
12.	Were they trained by a seasoned coaching program?		
13.	Have they been a coach for more than 5 years?		
14.	Do they have established online presence?		
15.	Do I feel that they are genuine and approach without hidden agendas?		

EMOTIONAL SUPPORTS

Your third base of support should be your emotional cheerleader support network. My husband and family, who only wanted the very best for me and were totally in for the long haul, are my emotional support base. While they are vital to the long vision of my business and success, and are a vital part of my very best life, they could not be my accountability partners to get me there. I will take time to explain what I mean. When loved ones see that we are in a state of uncertainty or feeling insecure, there is a tendency to want to fix the situation for us. There are times that a fix is the worst thing for us.

Think of the example of the caterpillar transforming into a butterfly. As the caterpillar begins to break the chrysalis, and emerge into the beautiful butterfly that it is meant to be, its not easy. They struggle as they unfold, and use all the energy that they can to break though the outer sack. If you were to see the butterfly and open the sack for it, the beautiful butterfly would die. Butterflies were meant to struggle as they exit in order to build the strength in their wings to fly.

We have to allow the struggle in order for them to become what they are meant to be. It is the same with us. If we are not allowed to work through some of the struggles that come to us in the process, we will not be able to develop the best problem solving skills that will be able to sustain us in our new life.

WELLNESS AND SELF-CARE SUPPORTS
And finally and most importantly, wellness and self-care supports are one of the types of support that are often forgotten. It is going to be important that you rest well, eat right, get adequate exercise and take care of yourself throughout the transition.

Sometimes I see people get so busy creating a life that they *love*, that they forget to love the life that they *have*. It is important to take time to decompress and detox not only your body but your mind. Do things and create fun and adventure in your life.

One of the things that I did when I made the commitment to myself about my Ethical Exit was to create times of adventure, and to allow myself to experience new and different things that I had not had time for before. I took a dance class and had a blast, I signed up to do a painting class with a girlfriend. I scheduled myself for massages and explored dreams of writing this book and teaching classes online. These were all part of my self-care supports that tapped into my creativity. I allowed myself the freedom to be out of the box and to enjoy life out of the box. As I began to play more and be more creative, my productivity seemed to soar. I found it amazing that the more I played in my life, the more I was able to accomplish.

As you go through the actions around your Ethical Exit, remember to give yourself the support that you need in these different areas. They will all work together to keep you stable and strong as you create your own significant life!

It is now time for you to get started making a difference in your own life.

For me the success of this book will not be based on the number that sell or any buzz that it could create. The real success for me will be that one person that will gain the courage and belief in themselves to act on their dreams and follow their passions. It is that one life that could be changed by reading this simple Southern girls writing. That will make the edit parties, the blocks, and the deadlines all worth it!!

I have to ask, is that one life to be changed yours?

Conclusion

Life is an adventure is a phrase that has always excited me. How you view your life is the paradigm by which you will act it out. If you view life as hard work, it will be hard; if you view it as a puzzle, you will always try to fit things together. For people who view life as an adventure, they may do all they can to inject fun and play and excitement into every aspect. My wish for you is that you can have a view of life that allows you the freedom to explore and create the life of your dreams.

I know that many of you have the same hopes, fears, dreams, challenges and responsibilities that I do – or you would not have made it to this point in the book. I understand that you still have questions, and possibly doubts, as to how you can create a life that you love and do it the right way. Hopefully having read *The Ethical Exit* has opened the door of possibility for you to help you clarify and explore your life launch goals.

For some readers, you may find that interjecting more of what you love into what you do will be enough for you to have the life you love, and that makes me so happy for you. For others, it may have awakened within you a dream that you had given up on. You may now see that you can do the work and take the actions needed to create this new life that you love. Some of you may have done the work, and are now ready to make your Ethical Exit. I would say to all of you, *great job!*

I hope – if this book has done anything for you – at the very least it has opened up your ability to dream again. If those dreams have been awakened, don't let them die, keep them alive, nurture them, water them, and feed them until you are able to realize them.

Your significant life is possible. That will be your gift to the rest of the world. I would love to hear your stories.

Acknowledgements

Growing up in the South has its advantages. Community is real, values are lived, and the Golden Rule really does work. The disadvantage to small town living is that there is nothing that you can hide. I grew up with the understanding that at any given moment, anything that you did could quickly become the café conversation. While I am not an advocate for such intense fishbowl living, it did have its lessons. The lesson that "right is never wrong" has never failed me. That is the premise that *The Ethical Exit* is based on. That foundation of always trying to do the right thing is as true for me today as it was when I was growing up in that small town. I thank everyone that ever modeled that for me.

As I have grown and learned, there are significant moments and people who come to mind having shaped me today. Some of them are no longer here to see what an impact they have had, but I cannot write without acknowledging them anyway. I know they are watching. To my "faux moms" Joyce Moore and "Joycie" Gibson I say thank you. You taught me that I did not have to always play in the box, and that sometimes society has silly rules. You also taught me some of the social graces that I still practice. No gum in church, don't brush your hair in the kitchen, say *yes ma'am* and *no ma'am,* and gracious truth will get you out of some real sticky situations.

To my high school English teacher, Dr. Gist, I say thank you for teaching me the passion for the written word. My Writing Good Sentences class has come in handy more times than you could possibly imagine. I also hope that you are not looking down and grading my work grammatically as much as you are reviewing it for content. And please don't let any of the angels yell down for a point if any mistakes are found.

To my mom, who always had a passion for learning new things, thank you. You were a strong professional woman before that was cool. You never tried to dumb down your intelligence or your opinion just because you were a woman. I learned that lesson well. You allowed me freedom to express and never got upset when I got into my creative mode and painted a mural on my wall or a diamond on my ceiling.

To my daddy, who was my Prince Charming. He taught me how to love unconditionally, to be generous with all that I had, and how to maintain balance even when things got crazy. He let me know that it is OK to listen to your heart, and do what you feel is right. Daddy showed me how to overlook opinions, and what it means to take risks even when others don't agree. I am your child and I know you and Mom are still watching!

To my husband Bill, and my children Jarrad, Justin, Ashton, Blakely and Jan, thank you for the privilege of being in each of your lives. You are all my inspiration. To my sisters and all their broods, you are all family and that means everything. To my friends thank you for putting up with me during all my crazy times. And most of all to my sweet Hadley and Harrison, you had my heart before you were born, and my love for you was the force that helped me choose my current path. You changed your GiGi's life and you didn't even know it.

I want to acknowledge my sisters and the influence that they have had in my life. You are always there and ready to be my biggest cheerleaders, even when you don't understand what it is that I am doing! The best times in life are with you and all our crazy broods!

I would like to acknowledge all the people that have ever worked tirelessly alongside me throughout the last 30+ years. I have learned so much from each of you. I have been a student of each of your lives. I watched how you handled the glory of the wins and how you responded to the bruises when you fell. It is those lessons that have molded my thoughts and actions. I was always watching your life in order to learn to become a better version of me. Thank you for the lessons. I still have many more to learn.

It was some of these very life lessons that I reflected on when I decided to leave my secure corporate job to share my experiences and coaching passion with the world. I was troubled by the number of unhappy people that I encountered in my world every day, and felt a need to make a greater impact for anyone facing the craziness of life. I wanted to help create a way for anyone feeling trapped to escape the rat race and create a life that left them fulfilled and having a feeling of purpose.

One of the most impactful lessons in my life happened when I signed up for my first medical mission trip. It was a true act of trust. I had committed to the project, and knew that I had been counted on for the medical team. It was then I was hit with a true financial crisis. I did not know how I would afford it, but I knew that I could not afford to say no. I was too proud to say anything, so I trusted in silence to follow my pull to a bigger purpose. A person that was unknown to me at the time was feeling the need to donate funds to support the trip. Those funds were given to me as a gift. That was a pivotal moment that I have gone back to, many times, when I felt uncertainty about circumstances. It has carried me many times. That trip changed my perspective on life forever. Thank you and rest in peace Glenda Garver.

I would like to give credit to Dr. Martha Beck for creating a coaching program that teaching authentic living that has changed my life. You were my launch pad for a new thought, a new dream and for a new way of living.

To my current mentors and team. Susan Hyatt who I have known since the days of Kung Fu Panda, Thank you for your support and kick in the pants to get myself in gear and share my work with the world. To my Mastermind group and Patti Keating for your help and accountability sessions. To my VA team, thank you for learning my style so quickly and for being so patient with me. To my publisher Angela Lauria and her team. Thank you for creating a process and a program to help me get this done! To my creative and talented web designer Janet Pashleigh, thanks for capturing my vision online, to Pam Slim for creating a group of Indispensables, and to my long time childhood friend Suzette Osborn who took the time to capture the essence of my fun side in my photos, thank you.

I believe that every individual is supported by a foundation, in the same way a house is built. If the foundation is strong, the house will stand through wind and storms. My life had that same foundation, and there have been many storms and lots of wind, but I stand today because of all of you that have made up my foundation along the way. Thank you for supporting me.

It is now my time to become the foundation for others. It is my hope that as you read this book, you were inspired to make the changes to create your very best life. I would like to support you, and become part of the foundation for you to build a strong and passionate life.

Please feel free to contact me at jeanne@jeanneboschert.com or go to my website and check out the support programs that I have created just for you.

What are you waiting for? Let's do this!

About The Author

Jeanne Boschert is a Master Certified Coach in Life and Business. She is an author, successful entrepreneur, and motivational speaker. She specialize in helping leaders, entrepreneurs and professionals discover breakthroughs in their personal and professional lives. Jeanne has spent the last 10 years of her career as a consultant in large corporations and has worked with thousands of executives, managers and corporate employees. She knows firsthand what life as a busy professional looks like. She now works to help them create more satisfying lives both personally and professionally. Jeanne is passionate about helping people to create a life that they love, both in and outside of the corporate scene.

Jeanne has been privileged to train and be mentored by some of the most noted coaches in the industry. She holds Master Coaching Certification from Martha Beck International. She has Life and Business Certification from The Life Purpose Institute and has studied at the Coach Training Alliance. She is also Certified as a 360 High Performance Facilitator. She utilized her coaching skills in her corporate role for many years to transition teams, managers and executives. Jeanne is excited to now take those skills into the public world with her custom Life Phase Coaching Program, seminars, retreats, books and speaking engagements.

Jeanne currently resides outside of Memphis, Tenn. She loves spending time with her family and great friends. She enjoys cooking, reading, shopping, writing and travel. You can read more about her at www.jeanneboschert.com.

About Difference Press

Difference Press offers life coaches, other healing professionals, a comprehensive solution to get their book written, published, and promoted. A boutique style alternative to self-publishing, Difference Press boasts a fair and easy to understand profit structure, low priced author copies, and author-friendly contract terms. Founder, Angela Lauria has been bringing the literary ventures of authors-in-transformation to life since 1994.

YOUR DELICIOUS BOOK

If you're like many of the authors we work with, you have wanted to write a book for a long time, maybe you have even started a book … or two… or three … but somehow, as hard as you have tried to make your book a priority other things keep getting in the way.

It's not just finding the time and confidence to write that is an obstacle. The logistics of finding an editor, hiring an experienced designer, and figuring out all the technicalities of publishing stops many authors-in-transformation from writing a book that makes a difference. Your Delicious Book is designed to address every obstacle along the way so all you have to do is write!

TACKLING THE TECHNICAL END OF PUBLISHING
The comprehensive coaching, editing, design, publishing and marketing services offered by Difference Press mean that your book will be edited by a pro, designed by an experienced graphic artist, and published digitally and in print by publishing industry experts. We handle all of the technical aspects of your book creation so you can spend more of your time focusing on your business.

READY TO WRITE YOUR BOOK?

Visit www.YourDeliciousBook.com. When you apply mention you are Difference Press reader and get 10% off the program price.

Other Books by Difference Press

Love to Lead, Lead to Love
by Janeen Latini

Fat Be Gone: Four Steps To Permanent Weight Loss And True Happiness
by Carleasa Coates

Zen and the Art of Making a Morris Chair: Awaken Your Creative Potential
by Randy Gafner

Why Is She Acting So Weird? A Guide to Cultivating Closeness When A Friend is in Crisis
by Jenn McRobbie

Sex, Lies & Creativity: Improve Innovation Skills And Enhance Innovation Culture By Understanding Gender Diversity & Creative Thinking
by Julia Roberts

Woman Overboard! Six Ways Women Avoid Conflict And One Way To Live Drama-Free
by Rachel Alexandria

Mafia|Kitten Lessons For Strong Women On Finally Letting Go, Feeling Safe, And Being Loved
by Valerie LaPenta Steiger

Tapping Into Past Lives Heal Soul Traumas and Claim Your Spiritual Gifts with Quantum EFT
by Jenny Johnston

Thank You

Thank you so much for trusting me to share my Ethical Exit journey with you. I know how hard it is to make a change. There are questions that could not possibly be answered in this short book. I would be glad to examine your goals and assist you in designing your Ethical Exit to your new life. I have created some tools as a special gift just for you to help you get started.

You can access and download those at www.jeanneboschert.com/downloads.

I have created several different programs that can help you to attain the life you deserve. Check them out here at www.jeanneboschert.com/programs-events

If you would like more personalized help? Please feel free to contact me at jeanne@jeanneboschert.com.

I would be glad to help you begin your journey!

www.ingramcontent.com/pod-product-compliance
Lightning Source LLC
Chambersburg PA
CBHW071725090426
42738CB00009B/1883